The Project Approach

MANAGING SUCCESSFUL PROJECTS

SYLVIA C. CHARD, PhD

Department of Elementary Education

The University of Alberta

CONTENTS

Introduction

Section I
Getting Started (Phase 1)

Prepare for the Project **14**
What relevant experiences have children already had?
Before a project begins, teachers need to determine children's
familiarity with the topic and check the availability of primary
and secondary sources for children to use as research.

Design & Planning Work **20**
*What questions are children asking? How can parents get
involved?* Fieldwork begins at home with children asking questions of parents and caregivers as well as one another.

Section II
Developing the Project Work (Phase 2)

Conduct Fieldwork **28**
*What strategies and techniques will children use to construct
explanations?* Teachers will need to provide new firsthand
experiences as children independently investigate objects and
resources, explore answers, and reveal new questions.

Foreword

The second *Practical Guide to the Project Approach* was written to clarify particular structural features of good project work. It was my intention at first to give teachers specific teaching strategies and techniques to try out in their classroom. It is, however, evident from my own observations in many classrooms that projects can take different forms once the basic planning structure has been mastered. I hope you will take the ideas and suggestions in the spirit of an explorer with limited maps but needing to chart more precisely the best roads to take to achieve your goals for the community of lively learners in your classroom.

Best wishes,

Sylvia C. Chard

Sylvia C. Chard, PhD
University of Alberta
Edmonton, Canada

Getting the Most From This Book

A project is defined here as an in-depth study of a topic or theme. The study may be carried out by individual children, groups of children, or the whole class. Project work is especially appropriate for children throughout early childhood and elementary education, but many teachers also find the approach helpful in teaching children at the junior high and high school levels. Project work enriches younger children's dramatic play, construction, painting, and drawing by relating them to life outside school. Projects offer older children opportunities to do firsthand research in science and social studies and to represent their findings in a variety of ways. Children have many opportunities in their projects to apply the basic math and language skills and knowledge they are acquiring through systematic instruction.

Structure The Project Approach is not unstructured. There is a complex but flexible framework with features that characterize the teaching-learning interaction. This framework is made up of the structural features of the Project Approach. There are five such features: discussion, fieldwork, representation, investigation, and display. Structural features enable teachers to set up projects that respond to children's interests and learning needs. When teachers implement the Project Approach successfully, children can be highly motivated, feel actively engaged in their learning, and produce work of a high quality.

HOW IS THIS GUIDE ORGANIZED?

This guide is a complement to *Project Approach: Making Curriculum Come Alive*. This book is designed to help teachers implement the Project Approach through its three phases, with particular reference to the five structural features within each phase.

The guide's introduction provides background information on the philosophy and methods of the Project Approach. The core of the book is divided into four parts. The first three parts each cover one of the phases of the Project Approach. Each of these parts is organized according to the five structural features of the approach. Also common to all three parts is the incorporation of case study examples. The guide concludes with an exploration of issues as they relate to classroom management. The following is a brief outline of each part of the book:

Part ❶ Getting Started (Phase 1)

In this phase of the project, children's current knowledge and interests are reviewed.

Prepare for the Project Outlines the role of the teacher during Phase 1.

Design & Planning Work Preparation for project work begins at home with children asking questions of their parents and one another.

Part ❷ Developing the Project Work (Phase 2)

During this phase of the work, children are given new experiences and research opportunities.

Conduct Fieldwork Discussion on meeting the needs of children as the teacher supports the learning and goals of the curriculum.

Implementation & Development Work A comprehensive exploration of children's involvement in developing their projects.

Part ❸ Concluding the Project (Phase 3)

At this juncture, children evaluate, reflect on, and share the project work.

Debrief the Learning This topic helps teachers determine when to conclude, expand, or summarize the work, based upon children's interests and enthusiasm.

Review & Share Selecting work to share is a critical aspect of the children's work during this phase.

Part ❹ Classroom Organization & Management

This section explores how the use of certain organization and management tools throughout the life of a project will ensure its success.

WHAT IS THE ROLE OF THE CASE STUDY EXAMPLES?

As previously mentioned, four topics will be used as case study examples. However, it is important that these examples not be taken as blueprints for projects. The purpose of the examples is rather to suggest that an observer could see the kinds of things described, but probably only some of them, in the course of any one project.

A Note of Caution Making generalizations about the Project Approach can be misleading. This approach to teaching and learning reflects each individual teacher's interests and particular expertise, and it is also responsive to the different interests and life experiences of children. Children living in the southern deserts, in the mountains, on a small island in the ocean, in the inner city, and far from the nearest town all inhabit different worlds and experience different cultures.

During the development of a project, build on children's questions and interests.

WHAT ARE THE FIVE STRUCTURAL FEATURES OF THE PROJECT APPROACH?

The following five structural features of project work offer the teacher the means to develop a *flexible* structure which is responsive to children's interests and learning needs.

These features of project work are described as structural features. Why structural? On the one hand, structure involves constraint as guidelines are established. Children do not simply do whatever they like. On the other hand, structure provides children with a framework that helps them understand what is expected of them. In this way, structure can be liberating as well as constraining. For example, children can approach their work in unique and flexible ways while working within the general framework. This allows different perspectives to be recognized in the effort to reach a shared goal: *the successful project.*

Discussions Meetings of the whole class or of small groups of children for discussion of a variety of issues and ideas provide a useful context for this guidance and sharing. The younger the children, the more valuable it is for them to talk with the teacher in small groups about their activities and investi-

Discussions help children identify what they already know, what they have learned, and what they still want to learn.

gations of real objects or materials. In small groups, younger children find it easier to maintain a conversation, and the teacher can more easily guide their thinking and help them to formulate their thoughts. Once a topic has been talked through in a small group, it is easier for the teacher to help those children share their ideas with the larger class group.

Fieldwork allows children opportunities to concretely investigate their questions.

Fieldwork Field trips need not involve expensive journeys to distant sites. It may be preferable to think of firsthand experience outside of the classroom as fieldwork rather than as a field trip. Investigating the school building and the yard, interviewing all the different people who work in the school, measuring and mapping the school: These are all examples of fieldwork and involve no expense for travel.

There are also many interesting features of their neighborhood that children and teachers can investigate easily. For instance, there may be shops, streets, signs, homes, yards, retired people, businesses, natural phenomena, buildings of historical interest, means of transportation, services, and utilities that can enrich children's understanding of their world and allow them to tap into specialist and expert knowledge through firsthand research.

Fieldwork provides personal experience children can use to build on their knowledge and to connect what they are learning in the classroom with the world outside school. Young children learn best about unfamiliar things when they can use all their senses to acquire new information through direct experience. The younger the children, the more important it is that the projects involve the study of things close to home.

When topics relevant to everyday life are studied, fieldwork allows the children to undertake firsthand investigations of places, people, objects, events, and processes in the neighborhood. While older children are capable of undertaking projects concerned with topics distant in time and space, they still benefit from fieldwork where this is possible to arrange.

Representations are the ways children express and communicate their ideas.

Representation Children can review and organize information about their personal experiences with the topic. They can discuss differences of experience or opinion and formulate questions to investigate. They can use a variety of representations in the classroom to construct interpretations of their experience — drawing, writing, using mathematical notation, dramatic play, and building models.

Older students can use a much wider variety of strategies to represent their understanding. They can review the information they collected through fieldwork and represent it in a variety of ways to enhance their own understanding of what they have observed and share it with their classmates. This is challenging—and rewarding—work for children: It encourages them to strive for a fuller understanding of the new information in the process of representation and to relate this knowledge to what they already know.

Investigation Project work allows for guided investigation of a topic using a variety of resources. Children can interview their parents, family, or friends outside school. They can find the answers to their questions through fieldwork and interviewing experts who visit the classroom. Children can explore and analyze objects, materials, or substances by handling them, sketching them, or using magnifiers to look closely at details and textures. They can also investigate further through books in the classroom or the library.

Investigations help children prepare for a variety of situations by discussing all possibilities.

Display In the course of projects, children can undertake individually chosen activities or work collaboratively in small groups on different aspects of the study. Bulletin boards or wall displays of the children's work provide both a useful source of information and a way of sharing individual work and ideas with the rest of the class. The teacher can keep the children well informed of the progress of the study by means of discussion and display. Display also offers children and the teacher opportunities to tell the story of their project to visitors from outside the classroom.

Displays are an important means of documenting children's learning.

These five features of project work serve the children's learning in each of the phases in the life of the project. The chart on the next page outlines some planning concerns as well as the characteristics of the beginning, middle, and concluding phases of a project. As a project progresses through the phases and the teachers' concerns change, each of the features of project work takes on new functions and significance.

Overview of Phases and Structural Features

	Phase 1 BEGINNING THE PROJECT	Phase 2 DEVELOPING THE PROJECT	Phase 3 CONCLUDING THE PROJECT
DISCUSSION	• Sharing prior experience and current knowledge of the topic.	• Preparing for fieldwork and interviews. • Reviewing fieldwork. • Learning from secondary sources.	• Preparing to share the story of the project. • Reviewing and evaluating the project.
FIELDWORK	• Children talking about their prior experience with their parents and caregivers.	• Going out of the classroom to investigate a field site. • Interviewing experts in the field or in the classroom.	• Evaluating the project through the eyes of an outside group.
REPRESENTATION	• Using drawing, writing, construction, dramatic play to share prior experience and knowledge.	• Brief field sketches and notes. • Using drawing, painting, writing, math diagrams, maps, to represent new learning.	• Condensing and summarizing the story of the study to share the project with others.
INVESTIGATION	• Raising questions on the basis of current knowledge.	• Investigating initial questions. • Fieldwork and library research. • Raising further questions.	• Speculating about new questions.
DISPLAY	• Sharing representations of personal experiences of the topic.	• Sharing representations of new experience and knowledge. • Keeping ongoing records of the project work.	• Summary of the learning throughout the project.

Overview of the Project Approach

Topics are selected by the teacher in negotiation and collaboration with the children. This selection can be based on the following:

- the value of the topic for children's learning
- the children's interests
- curriculum requirements
- the availability of resources for project work

More than one topic can be studied by children in the same class at the same time. However, different topics can often be aspects of a larger principal topic. This principal topic can suggest subtopics to be studied by different students or small groups. By grouping subtopics under the umbrella of a larger one, the teacher can monitor children's progress and provide resources more easily.

As part of the initial preplanning for a class project, the teacher brainstorms her own experience, knowledge, and ideas and organizes them in a topic or concept web. This web can be used as a basis for planning the project in collaboration with the children.

PHASE 1

Throughout the first phase of a project, a baseline of understanding is established and reviewed for all the children in the class.

Engage children's interests.

- The teacher discusses the topic with the children and helps them represent their own previous experiences of the topic.
- The children share their experiences with their classmates through discussion and displays of their work.

- The teacher finds out what experiences the children have had, how much they know, and how well they understand the concepts involved.
- The teacher helps the children to formulate questions about the topic.

PHASE 2

Sustain and maximize children's interests.

With the teacher's guidance children each become involved, working individually or collaboratively, at their own level. The children will represent their learning using basic skills, science and social studies conventions, and construction, art, music, and dramatic play.

- The teacher arranges opportunities for the children to do fieldwork and speak to experts.
- The children are involved in close, firsthand observation and exploration.
- The children seek answers to the questions raised in Phase 1 and ask new questions.
- The teacher provides books, research materials, and other resources for the children's investigations.

PHASE 3

Connect children's new learning with their previous experience.

The teacher arranges some kind of culminating event to bring the project to a close. In this way the children are helped to tell the story of their project to others outside their classroom; for example, another class, other teachers, the principal, or the parents.

- The teacher helps the children to select material to share.
- Through this selection process the children review and evaluate the whole project.
- The teacher offers the children ways of personalizing their new knowledge through art, stories, and drama.
- If possible, the teacher uses children's ideas and interests to make a meaningful transition between the project being concluded and the topic of study in the next project.

Getting Started

Phase 1

Project work provides children with ample opportunity for real discussion, decision making, choices, cooperation, initiative, joint efforts, negotiation, compromise and evaluation of the outcomes of their own efforts. In this way children's self–esteem can be based on their contributions to the group and to the quality of the group's efforts and its results.

Lilian Katz

Talks With Teachers of Young Children

Prepare for the Project

In addition to designing a topic web through a brainstorming and organizing process, it is a good idea for the teacher to think about the availability of primary sources of information and opportunities for fieldwork. The teacher can list suitable places for the children to visit and people for them to talk to either at the field site or in the classroom. A letter can be prepared inviting parents to help with the project in various ways.

The project will also require secondary sources of information in the form of books, posters, videos, etc., which may need to be ordered ahead of time for the study. Teachers who have been doing project work for some time will probably have resources they have collected over the years, which children can use to continue their investigations when they return to the classroom.

Case Study Examples

Throughout this book, aspects of the Project Approach are supported by actual case study examples. The projects in these studies grew out of the teacher's and children's interests. Topic webs enable teachers to use their general knowledge of the topic as a starting point for planning the project. When teachers begin with their own mind maps or webs, they become more invested, curious, and active about what they know and care about. Revealing this prior knowledge helps establish the disposition and tone for learning and investigating. Let's look at how projects develop by following these case study examples: The Supermarket, Water, Hospitals and Health Care, and Trucks.

WHAT ARE THE DIFFERENCES IN THE INTERESTS OF YOUNGER AND OLDER CHILDREN?

For older children, topic webs could be more complex and reflect more advanced understanding. The teacher of younger children should bear in mind the firsthand experience and simpler concepts that would interest learners. The

Exploring the Supermarket

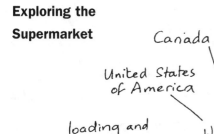
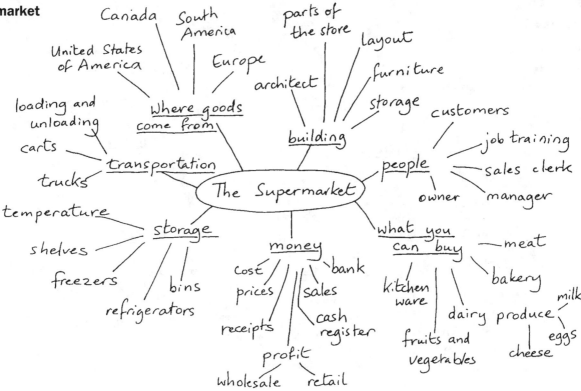

The Supermarket

Where goods come from
- Canada
- South America
- United States of America
- Europe

transportation
- loading and unloading
- carts
- trucks

building
- parts of the store
- layout
- furniture
- storage
- architect

people
- customers
- job training
- sales clerk
- manager
- owner

storage
- temperature
- shelves
- freezers
- bins
- refrigerators

money
- cost
- prices
- receipts
- bank
- sales
- cash register
- profit
  - wholesale
  - retail

what you can buy
- meat
- bakery
- kitchen ware
- dairy
- produce
  - milk
  - eggs
  - cheese
- fruits and vegetables

Understanding Water

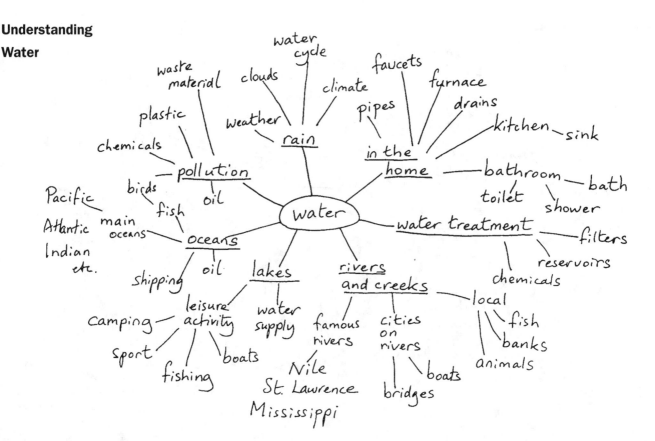

water

rain
- water cycle
- clouds
- weather
- climate

pollution
- waste material
- plastic
- chemicals
- oil
- birds
- fish

in the home
- faucets
- pipes
- furnace
- drains
- kitchen — sink
- bathroom — bath
- toilet
- shower

water treatment
- filters
- reservoirs
- chemicals
- local
  - fish
  - banks
  - animals

oceans
- main oceans
  - Pacific
  - Atlantic
  - Indian
  - etc.
- oil
- shipping

lakes
- leisure activity
  - camping
  - sport
  - fishing
  - boats
- water supply

rivers and creeks
- famous rivers
  - Nile
  - St. Lawrence
  - Mississippi
- cities on rivers
  - bridges
  - boats

Investigating Hospitals and Health Care Community

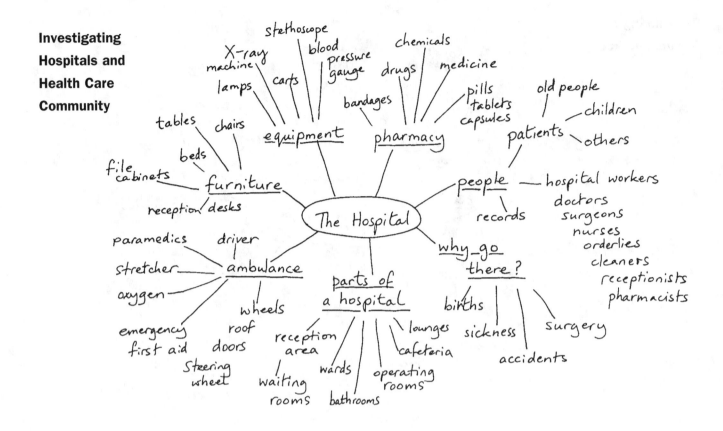

Analyzing Trucks

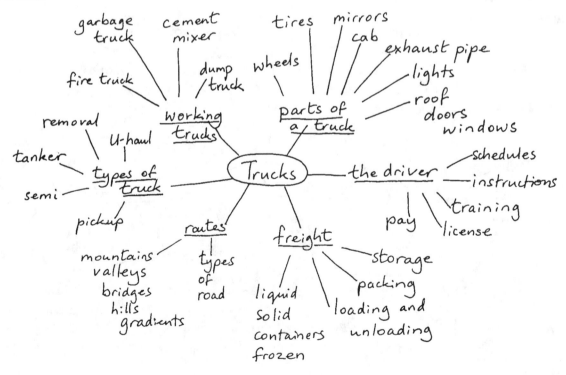

differences between younger and older students are particularly marked in the areas of understandings and skills. It is important to add a cautionary note here: *Any age group contains children who show a wide range of levels of skill and understanding.*

Teachers should keep in mind the children's previous experience, interests, knowledge, and the understanding to be acquired when choosing subtopics that would provide the most fruitful project activity. Even within one common subtopic the approaches and perspectives may differ across grade levels. Any subtopic could turn out to be important if children have experience or a special interest in it.

The teacher can collect books that reflect the curriculum concerns of the older students and books that anticipate the likely interests of the younger children. From picture books to advanced texts, the teacher can choose the resources so that they match the range of reading ability and information processing skills of the children in the class.

Developmental Differences

previous experience
level of understanding
use of language
investigative skills
representational skills
organizational skills

	PRESCHOOL/ KINDERGARTEN	PRIMARY	UPPER ELEMENTARY
SUPERMARKET	Layout, products, shelves, people, objects, money...	Prices, numbers, measures, plans, roles, functions...	Value, ingredients, boss, training...
WATER	Bath toys, rain, puddles, ducks, pipes, drains...	Rivers, plumbers, tools, domestic water...	Water treatment, pollution, conservation...
HOSPITAL	Personal stories, pills, babies, vaccinations...	Doctors, nurses, X-rays, equipment, bandages...	Health issues, blood, digestion, processes...
TRUCKS	Parts, size, writing, contents, driver...	Routes, distances, cargo, driving, repair, rules...	Maps, schedules, repair costs, materials...

WHAT IS THE TEACHER'S ROLE IN PHASE 1?

In the first phase of the project, the teacher should find out the children's previous experiences with the topic. An initial discussion, beginning perhaps with a personal experience told by the teacher, often awakens memories and stimulates children to tell stories of their own similar experiences.

The Role of a Teacher's Stories It is important for the teacher not to tell stories about exceptional events at this time. This may lead to the children competing to tell the tallest story, attempting amazing flights of fancy and preventing the teacher from learning the very information she or he was intending to elicit. It is also important to help children learn to value the everyday occurrences in their lives. For example, it can be more helpful to talk about getting caught in the rain than to tell about surviving a tornado.

For older students, the teacher can tell stories that reflect their more advanced understanding of how things work. Stories about routine things, happy stories, and even stories about things going wrong all work well: They

Overview for Phase 1

Teachers' Concerns	Key Events & Processes	Children's Work
• What relevant experiences have the children already had? • What do the children already know? • What questions are they asking? • What misconceptions (if any) have been expressed? • How can parents be involved with the work?	• Initial discussion of the topic. • Object to study, discuss and speculate about, story or video. • Topic web of current knowledge — baseline of class understanding. • List of questions to find out about.	• Recall personal experiences. • Represent personal memories. • Discuss and compare common and different experiences. • Brainstorm current knowledge and ideas. • Formulate personal questions.

serve to increase the children's background of basic knowledge of the topic. Use the chart, below left, as a framework for approaching Phase 1.

Case Study Stories

The following examples are outlines of real-world stories from teachers. These kinds of stories invite the children to think of similar experiences they have had. The teacher can offer simple speculations about why the first two stores did not have what she needed, why the water would not stop, why the doctor didn't give her the medicine himself, and what kinds of things can happen when you are trying to get from one place to another.

The Supermarket The teacher was going to make a meal for some friends. She found a recipe and made a shopping list. But she was not able to find something she needed in her usual store. So she went to another, which also did not have what she needed. Then she finally found it in a third store.

Water One day when the teacher was a little boy, he was playing with water in the bathroom sink. Suddenly he found he could not turn the tap off. Whichever way he turned the tap, the water seemed to come out just as fast. The water in the sink was getting deeper, and he was afraid it would flow over the top. He then remembered to open the plug. Then he turned the tap some more, and at last he was able to slow down the water and then stop it altogether.

The Hospital One day the teacher had a bad pain in her tummy. It went on for a long time. So she went to the doctor. He was not sure why she was feeling so bad so he sent her to the hospital. Another doctor who knew about stomachs talked with her. He did not think she needed an operation, so he gave her some medicine. She took it for five days and it made her better.

Trucks One day the teacher was waiting for some furniture to be delivered, and the truck was supposed to come at 10 o'clock in the morning. At half-past 10, he called the company and asked where his furniture was. They assured him it was on its way and should already have arrived. Eventually the truck arrived—a whole hour late. The driver explained that he had had a difficult time getting from the store to the house because of three things: 1) the road was being repaired and he had to go a longer way round; 2) there had been an accident, and the police had not been able to clear the road quickly; and 3) a long train had come and kept him waiting at the level crossing.

Design & Planning Work

The first phase does not usually last very long. A week may be enough. Artwork, construction, and dramatic play are likely to be quickly executed and impressionistic. The recognition of commonalities among the stories, shared understandings, and individual differences in experience enable the children to focus on what they already know as a class. Individual children's experiences of the topic may vary, but the collective experience of the whole class can provide a foundation of understanding from which to proceed with the study. Questions can be formulated and the children can make speculations and predictions, which can be explored or verified in the second phase of the project.

Informing Parents It can be very helpful to the children if the teacher sends a letter home telling about the topic of the project. The letter can invite the parents, grandparents, or other primary caregivers to talk over memories of the children's and their own experiences relating to the topic. Family members can also be invited to offer any expertise they have, to help the teacher arrange fieldwork, or to contact people who can talk with the children in the classroom.

The teacher can let parents know if there will be an opportunity for them to come to the classroom to see the children's work on the project. The teacher may write the letter for younger children, and older children can write to their parents and grandparents themselves.

> **What questions are children asking? How can parents get involved? Fieldwork begins at home with children asking questions of parents and caregivers as well as one another.**

HOW DO THE FIVE STRUCTURAL FEATURES SUPPORT PHASE 1?

During the first phase, the teacher helps the children collect a list of questions to investigate in the second phase of the work. Older children will keep this list on display so they can add questions throughout Phase 1. (They may also each accumulate a list of their own questions for later investigation.) The teacher records the questions for the youngest children. The investigation of these questions will be undertaken in the second phase of the project through the use of both primary and secondary sources of information.

Each of the five structural features supports each of the project phases differently. The idea of representation launches Phase 1 of the project work.

REPRESENTATION

The initial discussion can be just long enough for the children to exchange three or four stories of real experiences. Then the teacher can invite them to think of some ways they could represent their stories—other than simply telling what they have experienced. Once the experiences have been represented in drawings, writing, dramatizations, or constructions, they can be talked about, displayed, photographed, or collected. And their authors can be questioned for further details by interested classmates.

Help children demonstrate what they already know.

In the first phase of a project, children's representational work is reminiscent: They tell stories about experiences they or members of their families had in the past. Since memories are personal, sometimes vague, and certainly can't be checked for accuracy, the representations are not likely to be very detailed or elaborate or accurate. They will simply give an impression, with only the information that is essential for the reader to empathize and understand the story from the teller's point of view.

INVESTIGATION

The stories of their experiences children tell in the classroom are often much enriched by conversation with their parents about the events remembered. This type of investigation is a preliminary form of fieldwork for the children. They interview their parents, asking them questions about their memories of what happened.

Encourage children to interview their parents.

The children can become aware of the tricks memory plays, each person remembering details of an experience a little differently according to his or her point of view. Aspects of the experience that were fun for the child may have been annoying to the parent, what seemed a charming detail to the parent may have been an embarrassing one for the child, what was frightening to children might have made the adults laugh, and so on. Children can share these different perspectives in the class discussion. In this way, they learn about empathy and different points of view.

DISCUSSION

Reveal children's prior experiences.

The experiences the children have had both within and outside school form the basis of their firsthand understanding. However, it is important not to confuse experience with knowledge. It is possible for a person to shop quite effectively without knowing what happens to the money at the end of the day or how the products ever get to be in the store. Young children, especially, have many misconceptions. Some older children and adults are also surprisingly naive about many everyday things and how they work.

Scaffolding Children's Questions When children tell stories about their experiences, the teacher can ask questions to elicit the extent of their knowledge about the way the objects and people work. However, it is important not to "set the children straight" and give them the answers right away. Children benefit most when they can think about the questions and come up with their own ways to find answers. Inevitably they will have differences of opinion as they make predictions about what people do and how places function.

During a week or so of discussions of children's experiences, the teacher can determine which members of the class are most experienced and which are the most knowledgeable about the topic. She can also find out which parents are most interested in supporting their children's learning on this topic at home, which parents have special expertise, and which ones would like to help in the classroom or with fieldwork.

Project work helps children develop a fuller understanding of their own experiences. In this way, children begin to wonder and speculate productively and to formulate questions they can explore.

Case Study Stories

Here are some examples of children's stories of their experience with the case study topics. Following the story examples are possible disagreements that might arise and ideas for questions that might be asked to resolve those differences of opinion.

The Supermarket Children's stories might be concerned with weekly shopping for the family, pushing their own cart, and helping to find and even select the groceries. Most children could make an impressive list of the items bought by their parents each week.

• **Disagreements** These could center on where the money comes from that we use to pay for the groceries, what happens to that money, and how many and which different jobs there are in the store.

• **Questions** The children can be helped to list questions that may arise on a field trip to the store. The children may ask the manager, the cashier, and the people who pack the bags for the customers.

Water Children's stories might be about bath time and the different toys and materials children enjoy in their baths. The children might tell about getting their feet in puddles. They may tell about all the different things they see their parents do with water in their homes—washing, cooking, and caring for animals and plants.

• **Disagreements** There might be disagreements about how the water gets into the house, where it comes from, how it gets heated, where it goes after use, and how water might be used by firefighters and cleaned in water treatment plants.

• **Questions** The teacher can help the children list questions to ask a plumber or a firefighter or the local coast guard. Older children can make their own predictions about water pollution, conservation, and treatment and generate further questions to ask on a visit to the offices of the people responsible for managing the local river and its traffic.

The Hospital Children may tell stories of coughs, colds, and ear infections. They might also tell about shots and boosters, about accidents and emergencies, and about going to see newborn siblings.

• **Disagreements** These may be about whether doctors ever get ill, whether shots or thermometers cure people, or whether hospitals are places where you only go to be born or to die.

• **Questions** These can be formulated to ask nurses, doctors, patients or ex-patients, who might volunteer to talk to the children in the classroom or while they are on a visit to the hospital.

Trucks Children may not have had close firsthand experience of a truck, but they have all seen trucks close up on the street and in parking lots. There are probably a few children with parents or grandparents who use trucks in their work. Of course, all children have traveled on roads or highways, and older children will have ridden bicycles. Some of their stories may be about going from one place to another and what they saw or what they experienced on their way.

• **Disagreements** These may center on road rules, speeds, distances, size of vehicles, cost of gas, what the different parts of the trucks are for, etc.

• **Questions** These may concern the points of disagreement listed above. The children might want to ask a truck driver, a traffic officer, or a mechanic.

DISPLAY

Announce children's ideas.

Throughout the first phase of a project, the children can tell their stories using a variety of representational skills and strategies. The teacher can help the children share their work by displaying it on bulletin boards, classroom walls, or on tables and shelves. Displays of children's work can enrich discussions about the topic and about the representational techniques children used.

Allow for Variety From the beginning of a project the teacher can display useful words as a resource for children who need help with spelling. Older students' writing and illustrations about their experiences can be grouped in different display spaces by subtopic. Younger children's paintings, drawings, and constructions can also be grouped and labeled for display. Labels help children to learn about how to represent different kinds of experiences.

Photographs children bring from home can also be displayed among the writing and artwork. Dramatic play or three-dimensional constructions younger children make can also be photographed and captions written. Displays that combine writing, photographs, drawings, and other artwork and that have clear titles, subheadings, and some questions to engage children can be very useful teaching resources.

Curriculum Support   There is usually more language and artwork than mathematical representation on display in Phase 1. However, collecting frequency data on children's experiences for surveys may be appropriate for some children to undertake. For example, data might be collected to determine which children eat cereal for breakfast, which ones do household chores involving the use of water, which have been to the hospital, and which have family members who drive trucks.

Here are some examples of the kind of experiences that might be represented in drawing, painting, and writing.

Documenting Children's Experiences

The Supermarket	Water
• baby sister nearly fell out of cart	• sorted laundry
• helped with shopping	• splashed through puddle
• picked out favorite fruit	• sailed toy boat in the bathtub
• spent allowance on toy or comic	• ran through sprinkler

The Hospital	Trucks
• new babies	• family got a new pickup truck
• making people feel better	• rode in a dump truck
• talked to a nurse	• went to repair shop with Dad
• met new friends	• family rented a moving truck

Make a preliminary visit.

FIELDWORK

By the end of Phase 1, the teacher can begin to plan the fieldwork to be done in Phase 2. It is particularly useful to make a preliminary visit to evaluate the potential of the site for fieldwork. The teacher can then determine whether the site offers appropriate data and opportunities for close observation, interviewing people, counting, measuring, recording descriptive details, and sketching objects, people, and processes.

Meeting with the people at the site is a good idea. They may have some concerns about large numbers of children coming to their place of work. The teacher can explain the purpose of the visit and discuss some of the children's questions; they can also discuss suitable procedures for moving the children through the location.

This is also the time to determine who at the site will be the main guide and who would be willing to talk informally with small groups of children about their particular interests. It may also be possible for the children to be given materials or objects to take back to the classroom as donations to the project or on loan for a few days.

Reasons to Visit Site

- To note the items the children might observe (objects, people, processes, sequences of events).
- To become aware of the range of sensory data available.
- To meet the personnel.
- To see how the children's questions might be answered.
- To assess what might be brought back to the classroom.

Developing the Project Work

Phase 2

To give due recognition to the active and constructive role of the learner, a different mode of interaction is required — one in which the expert and the learner see themselves as fellow members of a learning community in which knowledge is constructed collaboratively.

Gordon Wells and Gen Ling Chan-Wells

Constructing Knowledge Together

Conduct Fieldwork

What strategies and techniques will children use to construct explanations? Teachers will need to provide new firsthand experiences as children independently investigate objects and resources, explore answers, and reveal new questions.

Once the children have shared their memories of personal experiences of the topic, established a foundation of current understanding, learned some common vocabulary, and made a list of questions they would like to investigate, the teacher can embark on the second phase of project work.

For the youngest children, the fieldwork is likely to be central to the study of the topic. The oldest children in the elementary age range may rely much more heavily on secondary sources, although fieldwork is still important. Fieldwork is most usefully timed early in Phase 2.

Once the final arrangements for the field trip have been put in place, the children can anticipate some of the experiences they will have, the people they will see and speak with, and the objects, equipment, and processes they will observe. Part of the fieldwork for the children will involve recording observations and information, which will provide a rich resource for the work of the whole class on their return to the classroom.

WHAT IS THE TEACHER'S ROLE IN PHASE 2?

The teacher's concerns center on the provision of new firsthand experiences for the children and the collection of other resources. Given the nature of fieldwork, teachers need to be prepared to accommodate the various learning needs and interests of children as a whole class, in small groups, and as individuals.

PHASE 2   INVESTIGATION AND REPRESENTATION

TEACHER'S CONCERNS

- What new firsthand experiences can the children be given?

- What new understanding can they acquire?

- How can curriculum goals best be met?

- How can the work be diversified to accommodate individual learning needs and interests?

KEY EVENTS & PROCESSES

- Preparatory discussion before field trip.

- Field trip.

- Follow-up discussion and plans to represent what was learned.

- Visiting experts.

- Long-term, multistage work.

- Preparing for the field trip.

CHILDREN'S ACTIVITIES

- Fieldwork: making sketches and field notes on site.

- Follow-up work: elaborating the sketches, writing and illustrating reports.

- Library research.

- Interviewing experts.

Implementation & Development Work

What new understandings can children acquire? How can curriculum goals be met? Field notes and sketches become the basis for detailed representation of children's ideas and thinking and help inform teaching.

This phase of work requires the most time. Children's work can take several days or even weeks. In Phase 2 children become involved in such activities as making books about different aspects of the topic, conducting surveys, making complex constructions and related diagrams, and conducting investigations and recording findings. This longer-term work gives the teacher more opportunities to work with children individually, responding to their different learning needs and encouraging quality in their work.

Most long-term, multistage work involves several subsidiary tasks. Not all these tasks are of equal difficulty, and children can choose when to undertake the most or the least demanding work, the most detailed or creative work, the most expressive or reflective work. This flexibility increases children's motivation to involve themselves in long-term work. And as their involvement deepens, the children look forward to completing work of high quality. Their pride in their accomplishment and in the effort they invested in their work is strengthened through this process.

HOW DO THE FIVE STRUCTURAL FEATURES SUPPORT PHASE 2?

The structural features in this phase of project work are used to help children develop their ideas and deepen their understandings. For example, during the discussion preparing them for fieldwork children can go over the list of questions they generated earlier. Reviewing this list will help children focus their investigations. The teacher can also review the recording techniques the children can use to bring the information back to the classroom.

The children can be given blank paper on clipboards to collect information and record whatever they find interesting. Younger children usually make letters or marks representing words or numbers and do simple drawings.

Older children, individually or in small groups, can undertake to bring back the specific information they are particularly interested in. Older children can also ask their own questions in addition to the class questions. Once children have some experience in interviewing people to gain information, they become quite active in seeking the explanations they need in order to understand what they are observing.

FIELDWORK

It is helpful to go on the field trip with enough adults to allow four (or five or six, according to age) children to each adult so all children get the chance to talk about their experiences. The adults, especially the teacher, can record information that may be helpful back in the classroom, as well as noting individual children's reactions and interests. The adults can also give the children suggestions about measuring, asking new questions, clarifying new ideas, and so on.

Children do real-world explorations.

While at the field site the children can be shown objects, events, processes, people at work, vehicles, materials, equipment, tools, machines, recording and measuring devices, plants, animals, and so on. The arrangements for the children will depend on their age and the nature of the location they are investigating.

One basic procedure that works very well for many teachers is to arrange for the whole class to take a brief tour of the field site with a guide. Then the class can be divided into small groups, each with a teacher, aide, or parent volunteer. Each group can then visit part of the site for more detailed investigation and discuss their observations with each other and with staff members.

Recording Field Experiences It is important for the children to have some means of recording their observations. They can record sights, sounds, smells, and textures in sketches, wax rubbings (candle, soap, or large crayon on paper of a contrasting color), writing, numbers, diagrams, and photographs. They can select the items of most interest to them. Once the children have undertaken two or three projects, they will realize that the quality of this recording—the attention they pay to the details of what they see and hear—will make their final work more interesting.

Case Study Field Recording

	SUPERMARKET	WATER	HOSPITAL	TRUCKS
WRITING	People's roles Produce Sounds	Sounds Sights Surroundings	People's roles Equipment Procedures	About driver Truck routes License plates
SKETCHES	Carts Checkout Food	Boats Things floating Fish	People Equipment Signs	Outside of truck Truck details Road/street
RUBBINGS	Wire mesh of carts Cart wheels Outside walls	Driftwood Rocks Tree bark	Walls Floor Textured mats	Tire treads Sidewalk Inside the flatbed
NUMBERS	Of people Aisle numbers Prices	Garbage items Trees Animals	Doctors and nurses Chairs Time	Odometer License plate number Gas gauge
MEASURES	Length of store Size of freezers Bags	Distance between objects Length of boat Steps around pond	Distance Room dimensions Wheelchairs	Length Width Seats
DIAGRAMS	Layout Store hours Food types	Maps Charts Water	Plans Rooms Parts of objects	Routes Timelines Loading process
PROCESSES	Packing bags Arranging fruit Stacking cans	Flow of floating items Water movement Erosion	Checking in/out Where forms go Getting an X-ray	Loading/unloading Starting engine Planning route
PHOTOGRAPHS	People Activity Machines	Canoe Bridge Water	Processes Objects Equipment	Scenery Inside a truck Driver
ITEMS TO BRING BACK	Bags Flyers Signs	Samples of silt Rocks Water Driftwood	Bandages Disposable gloves Masks	Map Blank invoice Travel guides

From the above examples it can be seen that field sites vary in the opportunities they afford children for recording information. It may be much easier to arrange for children to sketch a truck in a parking lot than a worker in the back of the supermarket. However, if contacted in advance, the adults at the site will usually be accommodating. Most of the sketching and field-note taking can be done by the children in groups (each with an adult) separating from the main group for short periods of time.

Safety Concerns In almost all field sites there are safety hazards, so it is most important that the children remain in groups with the adult to whom they have been assigned. Because children sometimes behave unpredictably in unusual settings, the teacher should set clear behavioral guidelines beforehand. As children gain experience in fieldwork, they become eager to channel their energy into their work. Teachers have certainly found the clipboard recording to be an effective way to focus children's attention on the purpose of the visit.

DISCUSSION

Children often have vivid memories of recent experiences. These memories may fade quickly; it is therefore important to reinforce them in discussion as soon as possible. An overview of the events that took place during their visit will help children recreate it in their minds and see it as a whole class experience in which they took a significant part.

Younger children find it especially valuable to talk about a shared experience. Children quickly learn that they each recall different things in detail and are interested in different aspects of the topic being studied.

Retelling the Story of the Field Experience At this point, children would benefit from retelling the story of their field trip in sequence—describing the events in the order they happened. They can also review their original list of questions in light of the new information gained on the visit. Both the teacher and the children can express their surprise at the comparison of the facts with some of their predictions. This discussion of the field experience will give the teacher a sense of which aspects of the visit were commonly understood and remembered and which were important to only a few children with special interests. This assessment by the teacher of the children's responses to the field experience will help when planning follow-up activties.

Two types of clipboards

Cardboard and paper clips in canvas carrier bag

FIELD WORK

Purposes of Discussion
- to recreate the event
- to review ideas
- to record and reflect
- to note surprises
- to identify interests
- to raise new questions

The post-fieldwork discussion can set the tone for the classroom work to follow, so it's a good idea to record the main events and discoveries discussed. The outline story of the class field experience can be recorded on chart paper, maybe in web form, and posted for children and teacher to refer to while the individual work takes shape.

New Questions Raised Finally, the teacher begins recording a list of new questions that the information brought back from the field inspires. Project work provides many examples of how answers to questions often lead to more questions. This gives independent research some of the aspects of a good detective story and involves the children in the pursuit of clues, further evidence, and new sources of information. Some of the new information sought can be found in books and other sources. Other questions can be followed up in further fieldwork or through inviting an expert to visit.

Experts Visiting the Classroom There are often many more people willing to come and talk with children in their classroom than teachers would imagine. Local businesses may welcome the chance to see the school. Project work is a particularly interesting aspect of the curriculum, and people are intrigued by the standard of the work and the interest, ownership, and responsibility that children show.

Gaining Support From Retired Adults Older people are an important and useful community resource. Children's grandparents and other retired adults may welcome the opportunity to talk with children about the work they did, their training, and about their hobbies, collections, travel, experience with other cultures, and earlier times. The advantages of having retired adults visit the classroom include:

• They may have more time to spare.
• They have a lifetime of experience to draw on.
• They may enjoy telling stories and are often very good at this.
• They are helped by contributing in this useful way to the community.
• Their involvement fosters good school-community relations.

Community Support There are bound to be people in the community who wish to be especially helpful and volunteer their talents and skills in order to help with the project work. In one project a maintenance worker built a section of wall with pipes and electrical fixtures to show children how these items function in the home. In another project, someone came and helped children to design and build different kinds of wooden bird houses so that they could observe the birds in the winter from the classroom window.

REPRESENTATION & INVESTIGATION

Following the discussion of the fieldwork it is important for the children to be able to begin work on the aspect of the visit that most interested them. This work may be long-term; children can make a book, an elaborate construction, or a display. This kind of work often provides the most striking products because it is accomplished by children who are actively pursuing their own interests. In this way, children contribute their strengths to the learning of the whole class.

Help children become the experts.

Interest Groups Sometimes a group of children may want to work together on something they were all interested in. A good way for them to begin is by discussing that part of the visit in great detail. They may then pool the information and elaborate on the recordings in their field notes.

Younger Children There is a considerable range of representational strategies and techniques that can be used by children at different ages or in different stages of schooling. The younger children can represent their experiences in talking, drawing, painting, modeling with clay, making constructions in sand, assembling block structures, or working with miniature sets of people, buildings, or features of the environment.

A well-resourced dramatic-play area can enable children to represent their growing understandings by playing the roles of people they observed in the field. Using a variety of props, the children can negotiate meanings together, refining them in discussion with the teacher.

The children's stories about their work can be dictated and written down by teachers or parent volunteers. These can be posted on the bulletin boards for the children to talk about with each other and their parents. Representations that cannot be kept or stored can be recorded in photographs or videos before they disappear.

Older Children As children grow older, they acquire increasingly complex and informative means of representing new knowledge and understanding. The following examples must be adapted by teachers for the children in their class according to their maturity and levels of skill. Each of the examples given here can be quite simple, moderately complex, or very elaborate.

DIFFERENT WAYS CHILDREN EXPRESS IDEAS

Art Events that children recall in the greatest detail are usually those that are most recent and that made the greatest impact on them. It's important, therefore, for children to record their visual memories as soon after the event and as fully as possible in whatever art medium they find most appropriate. Field sketches and photographs can form the basis of detailed drawings, paintings, print pictures, or collages.

Some graphic work can be done by children in pairs or groups. Often drawings can be done in the most detail by children working individually on their own ideas, maybe with a view to contributing these to a book or collection of similar representations in a display. Drawings can also provide some children with a basis for writing or making models.

Writing Descriptive writing is also best done as soon as possible after the field experience. Some children prefer to represent recent vivid memories in an art medium before they write, and other children prefer to write first. This preference can reflect an important learning style difference that should be respected by the teacher.

On return from a field site there can be several opportunities to write letters. Some children may volunteer to write thank-you letters on behalf of the class. Their letters can include new questions that have arisen since the fieldwork was done. Other children may decide to issue invitations to people to visit the classroom, answer further questions, and see the work the children have been doing since the visit.

There may be children who would like to begin their project work by writing a plan for making a construction, organizing information to make a board game, or writing a book about the most interesting aspects of the topic experienced in the field. On the whole, the writing in the second phase of a project should focus on the reality of the field site, on the way things are and how they were experienced. Expressive writing such as poems may be written at this time but are often more appropriate in the third phase of the work.

Mathematics Investigations often invite children to record detailed and accurate quantitative information. A variety of mathematical representations may be used for this purpose.

- Numbers can be used to label drawings, enrich writing, and help with calculations and measurements.
- Actions with objects can be represented with symbols for addition, subtraction, and so on.
- Part/whole relationships can be shown with words and number labels.
- Sets can be given word and number captions.
- Sorting is good for understanding attributes and categories.
- Graphic organizers such as a Venn diagram and matrix are good for showing comparisons, dichotomies, binary classifications, and relationships.
- Sequences can be shown through comic-strip drawings, flowcharts, and devices such as speech balloons.
- Frequency data can be represented in bar graphs and charts.
- Proportional data can be shown in pie charts.
- 2- or 3-dimensional shape names can be used to describe the form of an area or object.
- Enlargements or reductions help with concepts such as scale.

Diagrams or Graphic Organizers Can Take Many Forms They can also combine writing, drawing, and mathematical relations in one representation. They can be adapted to convey whatever information the child is most interested in. The teacher can help children to develop a wide-ranging repertoire of representations. The children can also be given various data-gathering forms that they can adapt for themselves.

MATHEMATICAL REPRESENTATION

Diagrams and Graphic Organizers

part-whole

numbers

comparisons

sorting

shapes

dichotomies

pie charts

actions

sequences

scale

bar graph

Case Study Examples	SUPERMARKET	WATER	HOSPITAL	TRUCKS
NUMBERS	carts workers checkouts aisles	bridges trees pipes sinks	beds doctors wards nurses	wheels mirrors lights windows
SHAPES	displays of goods packaging storage	in bridges pipes containers boats	buildings equipment ambulance body parts	parts of a truck loads and loading
PART-WHOLE	cart till store layout can labels	boat bridge house system toilet flush	stretcher bed ward ambulance	truck trailer cab dash
SORTING	produce cans packets people	boats pipes faucets materials	people instruments rooms furniture	loads lights truck types places

COMPARISONS	workers and
	  customers
	storage required
		boat types
		fish types
		hot and cold
		umbrellas
			ward and
			  ambulance
			doctor and
			  nurse
				large and small
				inside and out

DIFFERENCES	front and back
	hours open and
	  closed
		in and out
		above and below
			day and night
			sick in hospital
			  or home
				in and out
				moving or sta-
				  tionary

SEQUENCES	room temp.
	fridge
	freezer
	buying process
		making tea
		getting pipe
		  repaired
		river picnic
			admission to
			  hospital
			having surgery
				delivering
				day in the life of...
				loading up

BAR GRAPHS	types of goods sold
	food storage
	preferred veg.
		amounts of water
		  for...
		types of fish or
		  faucet
			surgery experi-
			  ences
			visits to others in
			  hospital
				types of truck
				vehicles seen
				  in 10 min.

PIE CHARTS	foods sold
	seasonal differences
	profits
		water usage and
		  time period
		amounts water
		  used for ....
			work shifts
			personnel
			costs
			time
				work types
				for trucker
				journeys
				loads

SCALE	store layout carts storage bulk buying	river lake water treatment plant	building ward ambulance routes	model truck routes traveled tools

Environmental Studies, Science, and Social Studies There are a number of representations that characterize these areas of the curriculum. Children are concerned here with what materials things are made of, what they can do, how things work, what roles people have, how people carry out their work, what procedures and sequences explain what happens, the interdependence of roles and processes, how things change or remain stable or in balance, what processes are involved in change, and so on. In exploring these questions, children can represent their findings in the following ways:

a) Maps and plans

b) Timelines and logs

c) Cross-sections

d) Sequence charts

e) Matrices

f) Flowcharts

g) Tree diagrams

h) Cycles

i) Webs and concept mappings

Many graphic organizers have precise mathematical content and involve communicating information clearly.

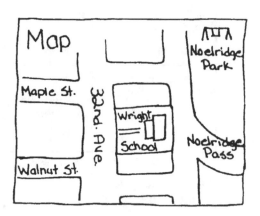

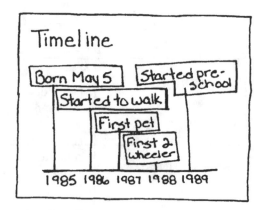

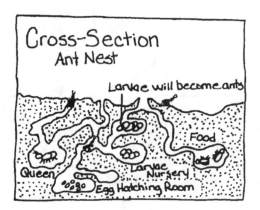

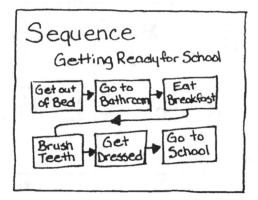

Games There are many different types of games that help children to explore, understand, and remember cause and effect relationships and factual information. For instance, games based on the principle of "snakes and ladders" (sometimes known as "chutes and ladders") can be designed by teachers at first, then by children, on the basis of interviews with people about their work.

Based on answers to the question "What makes a good day or a bad day in your job?" the children can design dice and track games that offer advantages or disadvantages to players when they land on particular squares. Advantages could be symbolized by taking a second turn, moving forward four squares, traveling up a ladder, or turning up a card and reading some positive item of information relevant to the topic of the game. Disadvantages might involve losing a turn, moving backwards on the track, or going down a chute. Cards turned up by players can also be used to represent a variety of information. The information used in such games is easily learned and remembered by the children who play them.

The games should be playable in no longer than 20 minutes and should be field-tested to refine their effectiveness as learning tools. The first games should be designed by the teacher. Once older children have become familiar with a few games, they can learn the principles of game design. They can then invent their own games to represent relationships they discovered during their investigations of the topic of study.

Music and Drama Children can write their own songs about the topic of the project. There are also many benefits for children in dramatizing stories of the experiences, roles, and processes they are learning about in their project work. As they play out their understanding, they see what else they need to know to create a convincing simulation of an event. For the younger children, role-playing is a very important and valuable means of representing understanding. The teacher can learn a great deal about the meaning children give to their experience by observing their play. Children can accompany their songs and plays with musical instruments. The advice and help of subject-specialist teachers in these activities is very valuable, and through such activity they can be involved in the project work as well as the class teacher.

DISCUSSION

Talk about and assess ongoing work.

The older the children, the more interested they are in accuracy, in getting their facts right, in making their representations correspond in satisfying ways with the real world about which they are learning. This developing concern for accuracy and precision can be encouraged but should not be forced. Children are at different stages in this aspect of learning and are easily discouraged if they are required to conform to standards of accuracy that they are not yet ready for.

Accuracy and precision can be modeled through class discussion. Appropriate examples of work can be shared and discussed so that children can more easily appreciate how they might improve their own work in this area. When children are encouraged to be curious and ask questions and to discuss and explore disagreements, they develop an interest in increasing accuracy, precision, and elaboration of their knowledge.

Discussion of individual children's work can take place with the whole class or it can involve only a small group, depending particularly on the age and maturity of the children. For older children it is particularly helpful if the whole class has a sense of how the project is developing and how the main concepts are being investigated and represented. Large group discussion offers the teacher opportunities to feature ways of working that might be helpful to any of the children in the class.

In small group discussions the teacher and children can negotiate and extend the standards of work. The teacher can also encourage children to consult with others who have completed similar work before or solved a similar problem by themselves. Discussion offers children a chance to ask questions, seek clarifications, and ask for particular kinds of help or new ideas from other children. Thus, several different kinds of collaboration can be encouraged by the teacher.

Discussion also gives the teacher the opportunity to teach concepts and to suggest modifications and improvements in the ways children are working. Project work involves many different kinds of knowledge about a topic. Children's level of interest will be high because of the depth of understanding they attain through the curriculum integration that characterizes a project.

Simultaneously, there can be representations of many kinds being explored and developed by children according to their different interests.

Children Learning From Each Other Children are naturally curious about their classmates' work. Although they learn most about what they themselves are directly involved in, they also learn a great deal from the work done by others because it shows them another approach to the topic being studied. Children do not usually repeat the same kinds of representation in successive projects. Most often, they choose to do work involving a kind of representation that they appreciated in another child's work for a previous project.

Children do not become overwhelmed or confused when a wide range of representations is used in the study of different topics throughout the year. In fact, they appreciate how the representations can enrich their understanding and how they can be elaborated to convey increasingly complex ideas.

DISPLAY

The discussions children have as a whole class or in pairs or small groups are an important way for them to become aware of all the work that is going on in the classroom. However, they also benefit from opportunities to study the work of other children more closely. One of the easiest ways to encourage children to study the work of their classmates is to display it on the classroom walls and horizontal surfaces.

Children engage in peer review of their work.

When children are surrounded with informative and attractive work by their peers, they are drawn to examine that work in detail. Sometimes the teacher can use a particular collection of work to conduct a discussion on one aspect of the topic. At other times the children can be advised to look at specific wall displays because the information represented there may contain technical terms or information that would help them in their individual project work. Captions can be designed to label the work in ways that invite a closer look. For example, the captions can take the form of questions or invitations to guess or estimate, with the answer hidden under a flap.

Displays of children's work encourage all members of the class to read, review, and evaluate the work of their peers informally. Displays offer examples of different ways of doing things, original and imaginative solutions to problems, creative alternative ways of showing how things work, where things come from, and how people carry out their roles in relation to the topic. In the work done by a peer, a child might find an example that clarifies a concept, suggests a new way of seeing connections between facts, or simply offers a technique that can be immediately applied in a different context in his or her own work.

Here is an example of a display in a classroom where the children are studying vegetables. It includes children's writing and drawings, reference books, a terrarium, soil samples, magnifiers, vegetables, gardening tools, and other items of interest.

Concluding the Project

Phase 3

Children are not plants with only one "natural" way of growing. They are beings of richly varied possibilities, and they are beings with potential for guiding their own growth in the end. They can learn to be conscious of the powers of their own minds and decide to what ends they will use them.

Margaret Donaldson

Children's Minds

Debriefing

What kinds of main understandings should be consolidated, and how? This aspect of the project provides an excellent opportunity to review and evaluate all that has been going on. The teacher will need to determine the children's interest in continuing or concluding the work.

After they have spent two or three weeks on the second phase of the project, the children will have learned much and done a good deal of representational work on the topic. The teacher must then make a judgment about when to call the work to some conclusion. There are several signs to look out for:

• Some children are losing interest.
• Some children are showing an interest in topics that are only tenuously linked to the main work of the project.
• All of the official curriculum goals identified earlier have been met to the teacher's satisfaction.
• The resources for firsthand research and investigation have been exhausted.
• There is a natural break impending in the school calendar, or the time left before the next natural break is just about right for one more project.

Some children will be eager to continue developing a project almost indefinitely. Others may be ready to move on. Sometimes children don't want to stop work they're enjoying because they're afraid they may not enjoy the next topic as much. Then they need reassurance. In any case, determining when to draw the project to a close is the teacher's decision to make.

WHAT IS THE TEACHER'S ROLE IN PHASE 3?

An event can be arranged that involves communicating, sharing, and presenting the work of the project to others who may be interested. The finished
product represents children's achievement at the point at which the work was
completed. Samples of the work can be annotated by the teacher and kept in
a personal portfolio for each child.

Phase 3: Concluding the Work

TEACHER'S CONCERNS	KEY EVENTS & PROCESSES	CHILDREN'S ACTIVITIES
What kind of culminating event would be most appropriate for this project? What kind of imaginative activity would best enable children to personalize their recently acquired knowledge? What kinds of main understanding should be consolidated, and how?	A culminating event. Personalizing new knowledge. Drawing conclusions and thinking ahead to other applications of new ideas.	Reviewing all the work accomplished on the project. Evaluating work and deciding on the best and most representative pieces. Recreating the project learning so that others appreciate the story. Imaginative work and fantasy in art, writing, and literature. Selecting the work for the school records and work to take home.

Review & Share

What kind of culminating event would be most appropriate? Children summarize and re-create their work in a form that best represents what they have achieved.

The children can share anything that can be shown or talked about at the presentation event. The main idea is for them to share their stories of the most important parts of the project so that their audience can appreciate the work and the learning they achieved. The teacher will sometimes join in and help with the sharing and sometimes let the children explain for themselves. It is important that the parents not only learn what information the children have acquired but also the processes of investigation they went through to learn the answers to their questions. The children can help the parents appreciate how they chose appropriate representations to record and communicate the knowledge they acquired.

HOW DO THE FIVE STRUCTURAL FEATURES SUPPORT PHASE 3?

DISCUSSION

Prepare for the culminating event.

In this final phase of project work, attention is focused on gaining closure and establishing connections to children's lives. The five structural features are aimed at supporting those goals.

Discussion with the children can tell the teacher much about the general level of enthusiasm for continuing with the study. When it seems a good time to draw the project work to a close, the teacher can suggest some kind of sharing event to celebrate the learning the children have achieved during the project.

Younger Children In the case of the younger children, a culminating event may only occasionally be the appropriate way to end a project. The children may have frequently invited their parents to come to the classroom and see their work. Also, the youngest children may have fewer products of their work to share at such an event. They are also less likely to be interested in talking to their parents about work they did at some earlier time. Some of their work, however, may be filed in a portfolio to give to parents after the project is finished.

Advantages of Different Audiences For older children, whose parents have not been invited to view the work in progress, sharing the project work through a culminating event may be beneficial in a number of ways.

In discussion together, the teacher and the children can decide on an appropriate group with whom to share their work. Maybe the group would not be parents but another class of older or younger children. For each different audience, the event will involve different purposes and benefits.

BENEFITS FOR DIFFERENT AUDIENCES

PARENTS

- Inform them about the work.
- Feature and celebrate the best of the work.
- Express recognition of the help given by the parents.
- Encourage parents to become more involved in the future.
- Explain the value of the variety of work done.
- Enable the parents to appreciate the level at which the whole class is functioning.

PEERS

- Enable them to share information and work.
- Celebrate achievement and encourage both groups in their projects.
- Let them exchange achievements.

YOUNGER CHILDREN

- Enable children to simplify and explain work carefully to younger children.
- Help children encourage questions and answer them seriously.
- Give confidence in public speaking to the shyer children.

OLDER CHILDREN

- Encourage understanding between different age groups.
- Help the older children appreciate work done by younger ones.
- Remind the older children of how much they have learned.
- Encourage the older children to listen with respect and patience to the younger ones.

TEACHERS AND PRINCIPALS

- Show the children that these people are interested in their work.
- Spotlight ideas teachers can share with the different classes.
- Encourage discussion of different representational strategies.
- Encourage all teachers to appreciate achievement at different ages.
- Reassure administrators that curriculum goals are being met.

REPRESENTATION

Select a form and medium.

Once the prospective audience has been chosen, older children can review their project and decide on the highlights they would like to feature. They have to decide on the most suitable forms of representation for the information to be shared. Several possibilities can be considered, and the process of choosing items to present will involve the children in evaluating the learning and achievements they have accomplished through the project. Some of this preparatory work can be done by children collaborating in groups, and some can be done by pairs or individual children. The event need not be particularly formal in character, and it is as important for the children to share stories of the ways they learned as to share the products of their work.

The kinds of things that children can plan to share with their audience include the following:

Songs, chants, and dances

Paintings, drawings, and other artwork

Constructions, models, dioramas, large and small scale

Displays, collages, and montages, all appropriately labeled

Skits or plays, improvised or scripted

Games

Writing

Mathematical representations and diagrams

Science investigations

Social studies information and surveys

DISPLAY

Display in the classroom has been described as having several communication functions during the course of a project. At the culminating event, the parents or other visitors will be interested to look at the work on display in the room. Some of the preliminary work of the first phase of the project could be displayed again to show visitors how far the children have progressed in their understanding of the topic.

Construct a classroom event.

During this phase of the project work, the focus is on using displays as a means of having children reflect on their increasing experience and knowledge. Displays become a classroom's living journal of work. They allow children to communicate (and celebrate) their explorations and discoveries.

INVESTIGATION

During this third phase of the project, individual children can engage in more imaginative or expressive activity as they review what they have learned about the topic. They may write poems or descriptions of unusual happenings, or they may retell people's stories from different points of view. In revisiting the information they have learned from unfamiliar angles, they check their understanding in a different way.

Implications of new understanding.

Some children may perhaps become involved in other work that is rather unrelated to the project but allows them to experience and practice a new understanding in a meaningful context for them. Even children who have little interest in the topic can become engaged in the project by investigating related subtopics and thus become involved at a different level. For example, in a study of houses, one child might be interested only in electricity and yet still make a useful contribution to the work of the whole class.

Small-Scale Individual Projects Rather than have children become bored with the project work, it is better to allow them to undertake some short investigation of a new and different topic until the rest of the class are ready to move on to the next project. Sometimes a teacher has children working on small-scale individual mini-projects alongside the class project that is being developed. It may also be appropriate for some children to experiment with their own poster presentations of the work they have done. Such children sometimes lead the class to an interest that provides the topic for the next project.

However, it is wise to limit the number of such individual projects for two reasons:

Reason 1

They can divert energies from the class project work.

Reason 2

They can be difficult for the teacher to support with the necessary resources to ensure the depth and quality of the work.

Classroom Organization & Management

The teacher's suggestion is not a mold for a cast-result but is a starting point to be developed into a plan through contributions from the experience of all engaged in the learning process. The development occurs through reciprocal give-and-take, the teacher taking but not being afraid also to give.

John Dewey

Experience and Education

Effective Learning Environments

What classroom environment best supports project work? Teaching and learning are interactive processes. These processes are best facilitated in a classroom with particular kinds of organization.

In the previous three chapters, the relationship between the three phases of a project and the five features of project work were discussed. There are also organization and management issues to be considered in relation to these structural features.

In *discussion* children have to learn when to participate and what makes a clear and effective contribution. When they undertake *fieldwork*, children have to learn how to collect data efficiently and how to select those items of interest that will most help the later development of their project work. Children can learn how to *represent* their growing knowledge and how to *investigate* new questions and interests. They can also learn how to select representation and investigation strategies that are particularly well suited to the information they are interested in. *Display* in the context of projects offers the children valuable information they can use in making choices and decisions in their own work. The resources a teacher makes available to children in these areas of classroom activity will influence the effectiveness of the learning that takes place.

Making Choices When children are doing project work, they are often highly motivated to follow their own interests and take ownership of their work. The choices they make may be small or large scale. Some choices can be offered explicitly by the teacher to all of the children, and others can be initiated by the children and negotiated with the teacher. This kind of collaboration ensures that no major choices are made by children without the teacher's support. Children are thus protected from making choices that might inhibit their learning while still being encouraged to learn from their mistakes or errors of judgment.

It is important to remember that everything that takes place in the classroom must have the children's learning as a primary goal. For that reason, the teacher needs an extensive repertoire of strategies for helping children make choices that ensure enriched opportunities for learning on a variety of levels. In relation to each of the five features of project work discussed in this book, there are organizational strategies that can facilitate decision-making by the children and thus help them with their learning.

DISCUSSION

Discussion with younger children is likely to be with an individual or in a small group. Discussions are usually brief, often spontaneous, and deal with the activities being engaged in at the time. The teacher watches for opportunities to involve the children in discussion as they encounter interesting or challenging experiences or come across puzzling problems to solve. In conversation with the children, the teacher helps them find words to describe their experiences and frame their thoughts, questions, and concerns. The teacher can also use a discussion to redirect the children's activity when it appears to be becoming unproductive.

Keep in mind the four learning goals: knowledge, skills, dispositions, and feelings.

Young children may need help looking closely at things, understanding the relationship of parts to wholes, seeing the opportunity to relate real experience to their dramatic play, or finding ways to construct models that will help them understand how things work and what they are for.

Discussion can be an important motivator for the youngest children. They can be given guidance and examples of how to use the materials and opportunities for learning in preschool, kindergarten, or first grade. However, if they have not had firsthand experience, it is difficult for them to understand through language alone. The role of the teacher is to be supportive and to demonstrate the options available in the environment.

Older Children In the context of the second to sixth grade classroom, whole class discussion can offer some important benefits for teaching and learning. Three main purposes of discussion are for the teacher to find out about the children, for the teacher to give information to the children, and for the children to share information with the rest of the class.

Purposes of Discussion

TEACHER EXPLORES	TEACHER SHARES INFORMATION ABOUT	CHILDREN SHARE
• Experiences the children have had. • The extent of children's understanding of their experiences. • The things they are most interested in. • The questions they would like to investigate. • How their work is going. • The kinds of help they need for their work.	• The topic being studied. • Limiting or extending the activities the children might choose to undertake. • Expectations for standards of work. • Procedures in the classroom. • The resources available.	• Information they have found out. • Work they have completed. • Invitations or requests for suggestions to help with their work. • Procedures they have found helpful in their work. • Ways they have solved the problems they encountered.

Throughout the project, discussion helps the children to reflect on the course of their study and to take stock of what they already know, what they have learned, and what they still want to learn. This involves the children in the evaluation necessary to ensure ongoing collaborative planning that is responsive to their interests and learning needs in each phase of the project.

Discussion can also be about the information being gathered by individual children and collaborative groups. Without such sharing, children would not benefit from the work of other members of the class. As children share their new findings they can also see what still needs to be done to link their discoveries to the project as a whole. In this way, whole class meetings can do much to set the climate for learning and develop a community of learners who can work productively together. The children learn to pool their knowledge and work toward a common and collective understanding.

Discussion Strategies Discussion can provide opportunities for children to share experiences they've had with different strategies for representation and investigation. These strategies are in themselves content-free. Once a child has measured periods of time and represented them on a timeline, he or she can use this skill in another project to represent other measures of time. Once children have drawn a map of one location, they can draw a map in another project to represent a different location, and so on. A particular advantage of project work is that children can remember and use the applications and the forms of many different kinds of representation throughout the year in different contexts. Giving them various examples and regular reminders will support and reinforce their understanding. These representational skills become part of a repertoire of strategies children can use at any time, in or out of school.

Group meetings of the whole class have an important function for the teacher in communicating expectations for the children's work. Of course, expectations will vary for different children, according to their abilities. But a teacher can inspire all children by sharing models of quality work that demonstrate work skills like devoting enough time and effort in planning the work, implementing plans, and presenting the finished product. These skills ensure work of a high standard in both content and presentation.

Discussion Routines Whole class discussion can take place at various times in the day. Some teachers regularly schedule group meetings to give children practice with a more formal exchange of ideas. Additional, briefer meetings can take place before or after natural breaks in the schedule, like recess or lunch. Within a block of work time, there may be a short break while the teacher reminds the children of some information, procedure, or expectation.

The location of the discussion group can affect the quality and atmosphere of the discussion. When the older children sit at desks they can take notes to remind themselves of things later. If they are sitting on the floor in a carpeted area of the room, the discussion can more easily take the form of a natural conversation. The flow of ideas that takes place so easily in an informal setting helps the children concentrate on the topic rather than on the rules to follow in a large group discussion. Sometimes it may be necessary to insist on the hand-raising routine for an orderly discussion, but at other times the contributions to the conversation can just flow smoothly as the ideas arise.

FIELDWORK

Fieldwork is an important part of many projects, especially for the younger children. The field experience children have in the context of a project is rather different from the more traditional field trip. For project work it is essential that some work has already been done on the topic (Phase 1) and that there is much work planned as classroom follow-up in the second phase. The fieldwork itself can be structured so that the children gain experience and knowledge in ways that will enhance their work in the classroom.

Fieldwork Strategies Children can be helped in various ways to take full advantage of opportunities for field investigation. Early in the school year the teacher can instruct the children in some fieldwork strategies so that the work outside the classroom can be integrated to enrich the work of the project in the classroom. The teacher often models the process of field sketching and making informative notes.

The first field experiences can be near the school or on the school grounds. The investigations can be small-scale to give children practice in observing and recording information in detail.

In the school building or yard:
• Finding items of interest—play equipment, fencing, walls, paths, plants
• Counting the items of interest or parts of them
• Measurements of the items or parts of them
• Making brief and informative field notes
• Observational sketching
• Photography
• Comparison of different items
• Noting attributes—color, shape, texture, function, etc.
• Sorting and grouping items in categories
• Making lists

Interviewing One aspect of fieldwork that can be a valuable source of information is the interview. At most field sites there will be someone who can talk about the place, the people, and the events in progress. The teacher can help children ask questions that will elicit information relevant to the topic. The children will also benefit from practicing interviewing skills in school earlier in the year. They can interview their parents to elicit their experience and knowledge of the topic. They can interview other children in the school who have some relevant expertise or experience. Finally, children can interview school personnel about their roles in the day-to-day running of the school.

Interviewing skills:
• Using polite opening phrases to request help.
• Explaining the purpose of the interview.
• Making a short list of questions to ask.
• Asking for clarification if an answer is unclear.
• Asking follow-up questions.
• Using polite and appreciative closing phrases.

The procedures involved in the administrative planning of the field trip will vary from school to school. For this reason, few details will be covered here. The arrangements will, however, need to be worked out in detail, parents informed, transportation arranged, money collected, adult helpers requested and briefed as to the details of their role.

If the field site is near the school, the teacher may wish to take the children back several times to record changes. For example, they may want to note changes to plants in the fall or spring, the construction of a building, or road repairs in progress. If there are opportunities for multiple visits, group work can be done across grades; for example, with grade two and grade six students working together.

Helping Visiting Experts Experts can also be invited to the classroom to help children with their projects. The children can interview visiting experts individually, in small groups, or in a whole class meeting. The teacher can inform the visitor beforehand of what the children are interested in and need to know about.

REPRESENTATION & INVESTIGATION

There are some organizational strategies that will help teachers to make choices about representations and investigations much easier for children.

In systematic instruction, an instructional method used for the acquisition of skills, the teacher often gives children clear instructions for carrying out a task designed to be done in the same way by all children. Helping children set tasks for themselves in the context of the project involves the teacher in a very different process. The teacher needs to see each task or activity as offering many different possibilities for children's work, depending on their different learning needs and achievement levels. For example, a book, construction, or skit planned by a group may take many forms. As the children plan, they work toward a final product that will be satisfying to them and of which they can be proud. Not everything in project work needs to be done to a uniformly high standard. On the contrary, some stages in the work may call for rough sketches while others must be done with care and in meticulous detail.

Making Choices and Decisions The choices children make in carrying out their project work should be from among genuine alternatives. Most decisions will have advantages and disadvantages. Sometimes children try to solve a problem in one way and later find out that a different way works better. Children should be allowed to risk making such errors of judgment and should then be encouraged to review and evaluate their experience so that they can reflect on how they might be more successful next time.

Learning From Mistakes In the context of systematic instruction, mistakes are often viewed as evidence to teacher and child that learning has not been successful. Children can come to associate making mistakes with failure. Life in the real world outside school, however, contains plenty of decisions involving risk. Children need to experience being both successful and unsuccessful in school to help them function with confidence in problematic situations. They need the experience of making mistakes or errors of judgment in a protected environment so they can learn the value of analysis and evaluation of the goals they have set.

Anticipating Consequences When children have experience in making choices and analyzing their own errors of judgment, they learn about the consequences of choosing. They learn to be less impulsive and more reflective in making decisions. They learn to make predictions on the basis of previous experience. They anticipate; they ask the question "What might happen if...?" At first, children will need help if they have not been making choices in their school work. The teacher can help by drawing children's attention to the possible consequences of the alternatives available to them. Older children can learn to talk about the advantages and disadvantages of different materials, time commitments, ways to collaborate, levels of depth or scope, and so on.

Supporting Children in Their Choices On the one hand, it can be helpful for children to learn about the consequences of making inappropriate choices. On the other, it can lead to disappointments if children (and sometimes the teacher too) are unrealistic about their ability to achieve personal goals. For example, a child might draw a truck she wants to construct out of cardboard and boxes. She lists the materials she needs to build it and plans the length of time she intends to spend on the activity. Even if she does everything well, the construction may turn out to be a disappointing achievement.

There are ways to help children avoid experiencing such disappointment. If they are inexperienced at making choices, the teacher should be available for consultation at each stage where significant choices have to be made. The teacher need not be there so much to give instructions as to listen to the child's developing intentions for the next stage of the work. Then the teacher can make suggestions so the child is aware of the range of options open and of their potential advantages and disadvantages. The more experience both teacher and children have with project work, the easier planning and choosing will become.

Organizing for Choice and Decision-Making Children can make choices in relation to their work. Some of these concern the kinds of investigations or representations they might undertake. The children's repertoire of these alternatives can be built up gradually with guided experience. However, many choices are simple and mainly involve good housekeeping by the teacher: making sure, for instance, that the children can appropriately choose the quality, color, size, and amount of paper or other material they need for their work.

Use of Materials Making simple choices is easiest in a well-organized classroom where the arrangement of materials makes clear what may be chosen for which purposes. In some cases the teacher's permission is required for the use of certain materials. It helps if there are clear guidelines concerning use. Certain basic principles apply here. These may vary but would probably include:

- economical use of materials and resources, minimizing waste.
- inexpensive and easily available materials where possible.
- recycling material that can be used again.
- labels on storage areas to indicate guidelines for use of materials.
- labels indicating materials for use only when the teacher is consulted.
- more expensive materials available for the completion of specially selected work products.

Choices About Time Where children have choice in how long to devote to an activity, it is important for them to be accountable for the amount of time they spend on their work. Teachers find that children are quite hard on themselves in their evaluation of their own project work. Like many adults, they tend to overestimate what they can do in a given amount of time. At first, teachers find they need to help children plan their time so that they are not too disappointed in the results of their work. As they become more experienced, they learn how to adapt what they are doing to the time available. They become more realistic and more responsible in the plans and decisions they make.

Depth Versus Coverage When children pursue an activity for a longer period of time, they are likely to invest more energy in it. They commit themselves more deeply to a successful outcome of the work. They take ownership of the work and can shape the direction it takes. With time, energy, and commitment also comes depth of understanding. However, the deeper and more detailed the knowledge involved in a piece of work, the less the coverage will be. It is not possible to have both. In project work there needs to be an appropriate balance across a variety of tasks. Children themselves can become aware of this balance as they choose their work options.

All children should have the experience of investing themselves in work of considerable depth and the experience of doing more superficial exploration. The choice of what to scan and what to study in depth may best be guided by the child's level of interest and the skills he or she can bring to the work.

These kinds of options can be carefully monitored by the teacher and decided individually in negotiation with the child.

DISPLAY

Display may take several different forms and fulfill different functions in each of the phases of a project.

Phase 1 At the beginning of project work, displays can help children establish a baseline of understanding of the topic through sharing their previous experiences. A class list of questions to investigate can be posted. Some basic vocabulary can be introduced or reviewed.

Phase 2 The display during this phase reflects the investigations being undertaken. Representations of all aspects of the work are selected for display so that each child can gain an overview of the work being undertaken by the other children in the class. The teacher can use the displays to teach from. The display provides children with models of presentation they can consult to enrich their own work.

Phase 3 The displays here provide material for reviewing the project and evaluating the work achieved. The work shown can be appreciated by visitors to the classroom as representing the story of the class project. Some children can experiment with poster presentations of their own on small bulletin boards.

Displays as Information Resources Displays have a useful function in relation to classroom organization and management. They can be helpful to the teacher as a resource for the children. Much of the information the children need can be learned by consulting the walls of the classroom. The children can individually find spelling and vocabulary references they need, representation techniques, facts about the topic, and the names of children who might be able to help them in addition to the teacher.

Quality in Children's Work In project work the child's time and effort, together with the teacher's guidance, can result in a quality of work that would be difficult to achieve under other conditions in the classroom. This media-rich context evolves as the children develop their interests and represent their learning about the topic of study.

Final Words

The five features of project work discussed in this guide offer the teacher ways to structure the environment for children's learning. Class discussion and display provide opportunities for communication and sharing. Fieldwork enables children's learning to be based on real experience and contact with experts outside the school. Investigation and representation are complementary means of learning that match the ways all of us can learn.

Message to Teachers The Project Approach can be implemented by different teachers in different ways. The intent of this book is to recommend strategies that have worked well for others. As you read about the ideas, be selective. Adopt those that make good sense to you, adapt those that may help you in your particular circumstances, and try different ways to develop your own style of project work. It is hoped that the suggestions in this book will enable you to experience the satisfaction of teaching and learning through projects and to gain a deeper understanding of the learning process.

RESOURCES ·

Katz, L. G. & Chard, S. C. *Engaging Children's Minds: The Project Approach.* New Jersey: Ablex Publishing, 1989.

Projects Web Site: http://www.ualberta.ca/~ schard/projects.htm